ROGER PRICE'S
ORIGINAL
AND STARTLING THEORY
OF
AVOIDISM!
A GUIDE TO DYNAMIC LETHARGY

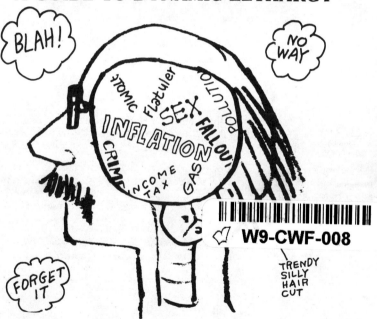

FOR PEOPLE WHO JUST WANT TO LIE AROUND

PRICE/STERN/SLOAN
Publishers, Inc., Los Angeles
1980

Other Price/Stern/Sloan Books
by Roger Price:

Droodles
Oodles of Droodles
Mad Libs® Series #1 - #10

Copyright © 1980 by Roger Price
Published by Price/Stern/Sloan Publishers, Inc.
410 North La Cienega Boulevard, Los Angeles, California 90048

Portions of this book originally appeared in Cosmopolitan Magazine Copyright © 1973 by Roger Price, and in Grump Magazine Copyright © 1966, 1967 by Roger Price. Variations of some of the material previously appeared in *In One Head And Out The Other*.

ISBN: 0-8431-0663-8

Library of Congress Catalogue Card No.: 80-65017

FOREWORD

The original book, *In One Head and Out the Other*, which thrust Avoidism onto a suspecting world, was published by Simon and somebody-or-other in New York.

This book is published by a firm in which I am a partner, and I planned to do it exactly as I wanted without a lot of interference.

Unfortunately, there are two other partners who outvoted me and announced that they were appointing themselves Editors.

They also put an announcement on the bulletin board with a lot of stuff about "accepting guidance" and "not offending the booksellers who are the backbone of . . . etc., etc." and "not cursing in front of Ms. Pollo, the typist" and "misappropriating postage stamps and paper clips." I didn't read the announcement. I also know nothing about the postage stamps. Stern and Sloan seem, as they grow older, to be becoming paranoid. *More* paranoid, that is.

INTRODUCTION

While still in my teens I began studying and analyzing everything. I soon discovered that we were living in an Age of Tension and that, because of this, most of my contemporaries were undergoing "Personality Breakdown."

There was no one I knew, except myself, who did not suffer in some degree from an Inability to Cope with Life or "Copelessness."*

In a commendable effort to alleviate this condition, I wrote a book called *In One Head and Out the Other*, based on the philosophy of Avoidism.

Avoidism was pragmatic, unique and a perfect panacea for its time. Since then, however, we have had a virulent outbreak of *Progress*. The culture has become even more unzipped than before. In the past 20 years, they (it must have been *them*, it wasn't *me*) have invented Area Codes, Ecology, Unisex, Skateboards, the PLO, Gay Lib, Inflation, Double-Digit Pornography, Cholesterol, Astronauts and Jimmy Carter.

*A word I have personally copyrighted along with "Droodles," "Mad Libs" and "Tiddlybakakawookingbubu."

Confusion has become the Status Quo. The invisible cord, connecting man's technological achievements with his ability to understand them, is already stretched taut and beginning to fray in the middle. As a result, we are still living in an Age of Tension.

I still am anyway.*

That's what this book is about.

It will explore the causes of Copelessness and other unrelated subjects and give you a first-rate means of combatting It — and Them — before it is Too Late.

If you feel it is already Too Late, read this book anyway. It will be cheaper than getting a pussy cat which would eat a 39¢ can of smelly food every day and bite your sofa.

---

*In a badly written monograph titled, "Puberty as a Way of Life," a Dr. Carl Gassoway claims that this is because I remained a teenager well into my 40 s. This is asinine and the man should be watched.

WHAT IS AVOIDISM?

Frankly, Scarlett, I don't give a damn.

—Rhett Butler

AVOIDISM is an optimistic philosophy designed to save us from ourselves. Avoidism is basic and uncomplicated. The Avoidist simply avoids things.

Descartes said, "I think, therefore, I am."

The Avoidist says: "I won't, therefore, I ain't gonna."

Avoidism is the ultimate philosophy because only by accepting the futility of existence can we have any Fun out of it. Sartre recognized the futility part, but then spent his life constructing a systematic justification for life based on the premise that there is no justification for life. I wouldn't imagine Jean Paul has had much fun.

For that matter have any Serious Thinkers had much Fun? Spinoza? Jonathan Swift? Frank Sinatra?

We should all make a rule to try and have a little fun each week as insurance against becoming Serious Thinkers. And as a first step toward becoming Avoidists.

WHY AVOIDISM?

Every religion, philosophy and moral guide so far evolved has proved to be unsound because all of them, from Marxism to Nudism, have been based on the same major fallacy: the idea that people should *do something* to prove that they are unique and probably superior members of a unique and superior group. Naturally, such Wrong Thinking can lead only from Anxiety through Frustration to Copelessness.

Avoidism tells you that you are perfectly all right the way you are. You are already unique and superior just by virtue of belonging to the species, *homo sapiens.**

Think, for example, how superior you are to a cherrystone clam.

Think how much more superior you are to the clam than the most important person who ever lived is superior to you. (See Table I)

---

*If you do not belong, send me $1 immediately, along with your name, age and, if you are female, a recent unretouched photograph.

MOST IMPORTANT PERSON WHO EVER LIVED

(Check one)

1. Julius Caesar
2. Albert Einstein
3. Leonardo Da Vinci
4. Napoleon Bonaparte
5. Plato
6. Roger Price
7. Jefferson Davis
8. Bella Abzug
9. Franklin Roosevelt
10. Atilla the Hun

TABLE I

You will see that the difference between you and any of the above is very slight. Now let us look at the difference between man and the clam. In order to arrive at a scientific estimate of the contrast, I once compared my cousin Clarence to an exceptionally fine specimen of Long Island clam. I conducted an exhaustive series of tests, and I append here a table showing the results, which exceeded even my hopeful expectations.

SUBJECT	CLARENCE	CLAM
Motor Ability	+12	+18
Sense of Humor	+40	+40
I.Q.	97	121
Physical Attractiveness	+3	+2
Ability to Remain Under Water	−53	+705
Neatness	−16	+83
Taste with Horseradish	+60	+60
Ability to Keep Mouth Shut	+227	−55
Honesty	−91	+100
Ping-Pong	+300	−300
Sex Activity	−4	+1
Political Influence	−15	−705

TABLE II

These tests proved Clarence's superiority over the clam beyond question.*

*One uninvited observer, a Dr. Carl Gassoway, claimed that the differential in Clarence's favor was due entirely to the inclusion of "ping-pong" in the test, which he said was unfair. This is destructive thinking. This man should be put away.

It is clear now that anyone is infinitely more superior to a clam than any other person is superior to him or her! Think that over for awhile. Once this conspicuous comparison is sufficiently impressed upon your mind, it will satisfy your ego, and there will be no need for you to prove that you are a superior being or a member of a superior group.

THE ARGUMENT AGAINST

Many reactionary, energetic, ambitious types will tell you that Avoidists are nothing but slobs.

ANSWER TO THE ARGUMENT AGAINST

This is true.

MAN'S FIRST MISTAKE, THE WHEEL

Once the wheel was invented, the deli-catessen store was inevitable.

—Roger Price

With the invention of the wheel, man began his disastrous struggle with mechanics, which has culminated in such technological achievements as the Neutron Bomb and the Frisbee.

I've put together a pretty accurate record of this event by studying certain early picture writings found on the wall of a cave located at 6 Rue St. du Pleisse, Amiens, France (second floor). These picture writings may appear incomprehensible to the layman (you), but they are really quite simple once you analyze them scientifically. I'll demonstrate by deciphering a sample phrase.

PICTURE WRITING (60,000 B.C.)
(Courtesy concierge at 6 Rue St. du Pleisse)

13

First, the round circle with radiating lines at left is obviously meant to represent a source of heat and light.

There can be no doubt that it is a drawing, crude but recognizable, of an electric lightbulb. This interpretation is particularly logical because the lightbulb was revered and worshipped by these simple-minded ancients as a supernatural manifestation.

The next figure is a little more difficult to decipher. It seems to be a drawing of some sort of growth, possibly a tree.

There were many trees around at that time, and I am pretty sure this is a picture of a tree, which these simple-minded ancients worshipped as a source of shade and as a handy place to hide in and jump down on passers-by.

Next we have what is clearly an animal, an elephant with a drooping trunk and a sharp, pointy tail.

Or perhaps it is an elephant with a drooping *tail* and a sharp, pointy *trunk*. It depends upon which way the elephant is going. It is hard to determine which way any elephant is going, as elephants are not much for going anywhere in particular. Regardless, I think we are safe in establishing the drawing as being an elephant, which these simple-minded ancients revered and worshipped although they did not even know it was an elephant. They called it *mastodon maximus*, obviously a pretty ridiculous name for an elephant.

We come to the final drawing, a representation of the early Cro-Magnon god, Owww, the god of Tooth Decay.

This god wielded great influence among the Cro-Magnons because if something happened to their teeth, they were unable to eat or bite anyone.

Now, having deciphered, singly, each of the pictures in this cave-wall inscription, we are able to read the brief but dramatic message that some long-forgotten artist left for posterity.

According to my notes, this message seems to be: "Leave an electric light in the tree so the elephant can find his way home from the dentist's office." Then again it could be translated literally: "Leave an elephant in the tree so the electric light can find its way home from the dentist's office."

There is one further translation that can be justified from a careful study of these symbols. That translation, which I personally lean toward, is: *"No Smoking!"*

It is from a long study of such prehistoric scribblings that I was able to piece together the story of the wheel.

Once upon a time, there was a cliff dweller named Marvin Ouk. Marvin was short, squat, barrel-chested, prognathous, and insolvent. He gave off the strong and unmistakable scent of Italian sausage and had five-o'clock shadow all over. He was, in a word, a fine specimen of his race.

These primitive savages had already begun to develop an unnatural non-avoidistic society, and with their customs they laid the foundation for the social systems of the present day.

One person was selected from the tribe to be the Chief, or "Momser," and everyone else in the tribe had to do exactly as he said or, in conformance with their system of religious taboos, he would break their backs.

The selection of the Chief was also similar to contemporary procedure. Anyone in the tribe was eligible to become Chief. All he had to do was whip the existing Chief in a fight.

The business of challenging and fighting the Chief was conducted very formally, and the challenger could use only those tactics sanctioned by the tribe's Code of Fair Play: Slipping-Up-Behind-and-Crushing-Skull-With-Ax; Slitting-Throat-While-Asleep; or Dropping-Big-Boulder-From-Ambush.

Now, the Chief of Marvin Ouk's tribe was an older man, a retired rock knocker named Jarge the Moose. Marvin was jealous of Jarge the Moose because Jarge had 22 wives. Marvin's jealousy was somewhat heightened by the fact that there were only 22 women in the tribe.

Marvin finally decided he had to do something so that he could get a wife. He decided that there were two ways he could get one of Jarge the Moose's wives for himself. One was by fighting Jarge. He decided against this, for obvious reasons. (See below)

(Scale: 1 inch equals 4 feet)

So he decided on the second way. He would steal one of the wives (the third from the left) and run away with her. He knew that if he wanted to get away safely, he wouldn't be able to carry the wife, he would have to take her in a wagon, and he would have to have a very fast wagon.

Now, in those days, no one knew anything about wagon technology and all wagons looked like this:

WAGON (BEFORE MARVIN OUK)

These wagons didn't go very fast. So Marvin began to think about ways to make his wagon go faster. He finally got some rubbery substance from a gum tree and molded it into the shape of a tire. But it wouldn't fit the squares on his wagon, and kept springing into a shape like this:

After a month or two of wondering what to do about this, Marvin thought of hacking the corners off the square, and developed a shape like this:

which was the first wheel! He put this wheel on the left rear axle of his wagon, and it worked fine. He got much more speed out of this wheel.

Later, Marvin thought of hacking off the corners of the other three squares and wound up with four wheels on his wagon, which now was 20 times as fast as any other wagon in the tribe.

As a result of Marvin's cleverness, ambition, and ingenuity, the Chief, Jarge the Moose, broke Marvin's back and took the wagon for his own use, and he and his 22 wives lived happily ever after.

So much for the wheel.

BASIC TRAINING

—*Johann Sebastian Bach*

Becoming a Born Again Avoidist is easier than becoming a Jesuit or a Dallas Cowboy cheerleader. You don't need a Calling or a Big Bust. But some preparation is required to un-condition yourself and dampen endocrine activity.

The first rule is Start Slowly. Do not try to go "cold turkey" by avoiding rock music, television or automobile driving right away.

Following are a few warm-up exercises, things you can successfully avoid with a minimum of torpor.
 — *Climbing Mt. McKinley barefoot*
 — *Becoming Prime Minister of Nicaragua*
 — *Writing a fan letter to Billy Carter*
 — *Phoning the Preparation H Company and telling them what they can do with their product*
 — *Crossing the Atlantic Ocean in a canoe*

Now that you have built up your lack of confidence you may move along to the avoidance of things which require a little more listlessness.

1. Luncheon checks.
2. In-laws.
3. Junk mail.
4. Appointments to do something.

There are a number of USEFUL PHRASES that will come in very handy and help you with Number 4. Learn these phrases and use them selectively.

10 USEFUL PHRASES

(Each phrase is preceded by "I can't because ... ")
1. I don't drive.
2. I am afraid to fly in airplanes.
3. I have to report to my parole officer every Thursday.
4. I have a piano lesson.
5. I just shorted out my Pace Maker.
6. I'm in alpha wave therapy.
7. I think I have bubonic plague.
8. my leisure suit is at the cleaners.
9. I am late for my Yoga class.
10. my foot is nervous.

Once you have practiced all of the above for two hours or less, you will be ready for more serious training.

Below are illustrated the Basic Position (A) and several variations, all invaluable to the Novice.

POSITION A

(Basic Position)

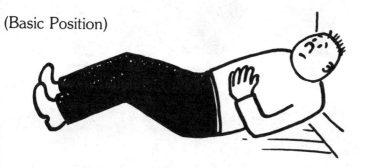

POSITION B

(Position suitable for watching unplugged television set)

POSITION C

(A Fun position, useful when avoiding Bill Collectors and Ex-Wives.)

POSITION D

(Avoidist avoiding using deodorant.)

POSITION E

(Slope's Stoop. Useful for avoiding conversation at parties. Avoid this position if other guests can be described as "playful.")

Practice these positions several (at least 10) hours a day until you have mastered them. Do not be impatient. Remember, "Easily learned, easily forgotten." The Novice Avoidist should spend at least a month on the Basic positions. Then, and not before, you may go on to the advanced Avoidist Position.

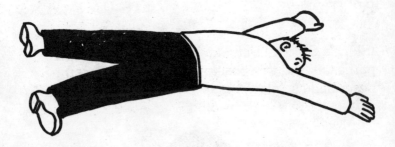

POSITION F (ADVANCED— Not for beginners.)

While practicing this position, you may meditate about various aspects of modern culture and counter-culture which you feel you can do without. Here are a few to help you get started:

—*Canned diet shakes that taste like wallpaper paste*
—*Movies that show violence in slow motion*
—*Checks printed over a full color reproduction of The Last Supper*
—*Air Fresheners that smell like condemned cantaloupe*
—*Gossip magazines with Rock Singers on cover.*
—*Fat French Fries*
—*People who use the word "sick" to describe everything they don't like*
—*Any book by any politician*
—*Disco tunes that have the drum carrying the melody*
—*The Gabors*

—*Oral Roberts, Billy Graham and all Sunday Morning Telecasts.*
—*People who Smoke.*
—*People who object to other people smoking.*
—*People who sneak grapefruit rinds and old coffee grounds into the pockets of your (my) new double knit jacket.*
—*Dr. Carl Gassoway*
—*Four-acre supermarkets with only three check-out counters.*

You are now ready to join the local Action Committee, obtain membership in the General Avoidist Disassociation and receive your membership button – a chrome-plated Valium Tablet.

ANOTHER REASON (BELOW) FOR US ALL TO BECOME AVOIDISTS QUICK

In a recent issue of the National Enquirer, which bills itself as having the "largest circulation of any paper in America," the following Headlines were on the Cover Page:

BOY CAN SEE WITH HIS EARS

ALIEN FROM SPACE SHARES WOMAN'S MIND AND BODY, HYPNOSIS REVEALS

JACLYN AND CHERYL UNHAPPY WITH NEW CHARLIE'S ANGEL

USE YOUR HOROSCOPE TO FIGHT INFLATION

and

FAST FOODS ARE GOOD FOR YOU

APPLIED
AND ACTIVE AVOIDISM

I charge thee, fling away ambition, By that sin fell the angels.
— *Shakespeare*
KING HENRY VIII, Act III

In November of 1975, the GAD Strategy Board, meeting in closed session at the Sherman Oaks, CA. Avoidatorium and Frozen Yogurt Store, drew up a list of certain key industries and made plans to infiltrate and organize the non-workers in these fields. The results have been encouraging.

As of July 26, 1979, Avoidist Membership Cards were held by 79% of all Government workers. This elite group has its Headquarters in Washington and its own slogan: "The buck doesn't stop here!"

Next in importance are secretaries, receptionists, and telephone company employees. Once we enroll 80% of this last group we will hold a giant Avoidist demonstration by putting the entire country on "Hold" for 24 hours.

BUSINESS AVOIDING

If you are a businessman you can use Avoidism to upgrade your position in the Organization by creating an Executive Image for yourself. To do this you must do two things:

(1) Convince everyone that you are a Decision Maker.

(2) Never make a decision.

This can be done by using the Avoidist figure of speech known as the CATEGORIC TENTATIVE. Say things such as:

"Absolutely perhaps"
"Positively maybe"
"Definitely either yes or no" and
"Comme ci, comme ca" (if you are a snob).

Of course, occasionally you will be confronted with a real problem. When this happens bring up a bigger problem. For instance, if you are a production manager and someone rushes in and says "Harry, the last 1400 bottles came off the assembly line upside down," you say, "Charley, I understand your secretary is pregnant," then put your arm on his shoulder and walk him out of your office.

Or if you're a Marketing V.P. and at a Staff Meeting the president says, "Harry, sales in your division were off 88% last month," you stand up at once and announce that the Plant is on fire.

For further information send for Pamphlets 5446/d HOW TO SET THE PLANT ON FIRE and 5446/e, HOW TO GET CHARLEY'S SECRETARY PREGNANT.

POLITICAL AVOIDISM or HOW TO SURVIVE YET ANOTHER ELECTION

Politically, Americans seem to have embraced the principals of Avoidism with an encouraging lack of enthusiasm. In local elections it is considered a phenomenon if 25% of the eligible voters turn out. In the last national election (can you remember who ran against what's-his-name?) 55% of the citizens who were entitled to vote ignored the whole thing. We are rapidly losing interest in the succession of clowns, nonentities, opportunists and fourth-rate personalities who blather at us every four years.

We look forward to the time when this antipathy will become so complete that absolutely no one will vote in an election except the candidates.

HISTORY OF MOVEMENT

Avarice, ambition, lust etc. are nothing but species of madness, although not enumerated among diseases.

—Spinoza

Back in 1907, two brothers were running a bicycle repair shop in Ohio. One day, Wilbur, one of the brothers, was looking out the window and happened to see a swallow soaring effortlessly through the air. He called his brother to the window. "Orville," he said, "someday men will fly through the air like that bird." A speculative gleam came into Orville's eyes, the beginnings of a dream. And seven years later, those two brothers, Orville and Wilbur Hammerslip, were bankrupt.

They wasted no time trying to invent a flying machine. They avoided the whole ridiculous idea. (And if two other brothers from the same Ohio town had only done the same, the world would be better off today.)

EXAMPLES of Avoidism such as this exist throughout the whole of recorded history. In every century we find certain avant-garde thinkers who have tried to establish an island of sanity around themselves. But with no organized plan, their efforts were doomed to failure. I have documented five examples for you to study.

Ptolemy I. In the forty-eighth century B.C., Ptolemy, of the tribe of Sneferu, was Master and King of the fertile valley of the Nile and of Egypt. Adversity and unrest were absent from the land, there being no crop shortages, droughts, pestilences or television news programs.

The people, lacking nothing, were contented; they enjoyed prosperity and peace. So did Ptolemy. One day, Barkal, Chief Adviser to Ptolemy, produced himself before the King and spoke at length, finally saying, "O Mighty King, things are pretty quiet around here. The people got a lot of extra time on their hands. Why don't we get a 100,000 men and spend the next 50 years dragging huge stones from an unknown source and lift them into place by some mysterious method and erect a "gigantic" pyramid, utilizing engineering principles that the most brilliant minds of future generations will not be able to fathom?"

This statement being of the greatest complexity, it took some time before it became clear to Ptolemy, who then answered Barkal by saying, "A Pyramid, eh? Why should I build a Pyramid?"

To which Barkal replied, "Because it's not there."

Ptolemy, seeing no virtue in the plan, had Barkal executed and the whole thing was forgotten until some years later when it was revived by Ptolemy's great-grandson Khufu, who was sold a package deal which included a Sphinx.

—*Plutarch's Lives (A.D. 95)*

Charles Cornwallis, First Marquis (1738-1805), eldest son of Charles, first Earl Cornwallis (1700-62), was educated at Eton. He entered the British Army and served in Germany in 1761, where he first practiced crude attempts at amateur avoiding. He fought as major general against the Americans in their war for Independence and by a series of shrewd errors in judgment managed to avoid winning decisive engagements including the battle of Yorktown in 1781.

—From the *Encyclopedia Britannica,* Vol. 6

Austrian songwriter Franz Schubert became interested in Avoiding while in the middle of writing a symphony, which he suddenly stopped work on and never finished. (Pianoforte, Harpsichord, Clavier, Organ, Copying, Arranging. Will travel.)

—Musician's Directory for 1810—
Vienna Local 408 (AF of L)

P.P.P. Eater. Peter Peter Pumkin Eater had a wife and couldn't keep her. He put her in a pumpkin shell, and there he kept her very well.

—From a collection of Psychopathic Histories published in 1854 by M. Goose

CLAYTON SLOPE

AN APPRECIATION

The father of modern Avoidism, or at least the inspiration for much of it, is Clayton Slope, a friend of J. Taylor Dorsey's, who is thought to be a cousin of my Aunt Diocletian.

There was something about Clayton's weak, watery stare, the shifty set of his tiny chin, the way his small shoulders slumped forward, almost touching across his narrow chest, that fascinated me. I am sure that Boswell must have felt a similar sense of fate when he first chanced upon Doctor Johnson.

Clayton Slope, although he did not know the word, was destined from the start to be an Avoidist. He was an 11-month baby.

Clayton was best known for his clever way of making any conceivable sentence sound like: "I had one grunch, but the eggplant over there!"

He was the most avoidable man I ever saw.

Clayton Slope is devoting his life to the ideals of Avoidism. He has not become an executive with General Motors or comptroller of AT&T. He has avoided the trap of heading up a Presidential commission to study the environmental factors related to the production of Krazy Glue. He has also avoided changing his socks (he occasionally puts Tic-Tacs in his shoes), learning to read and spending a holiday on the Costa del Sol.

Before starting this book I paid him a visit and asked him if he had any message for the new generation of American Avoidists. He thought for some time, then looked up, nodded and said, "I had one grunch, but the eggplant over there."

I am sure that we can all agree with that.

THE WORKINGS OF THE HUMAN MIND IN THE HEAD

It is an honor for a man to cease from strife; but every fool will be meddling.

—BIBLE, Proverbs 20:3

To fully understand Copelessness we must understand the workings of the Human Mind in the Head.

Let us take up first the allegedly "normal" Human Mind, starting with the overall picture. I have drawn this picture, showing the entire central nervous system of the average male and the internal parts of the body that relate to it.

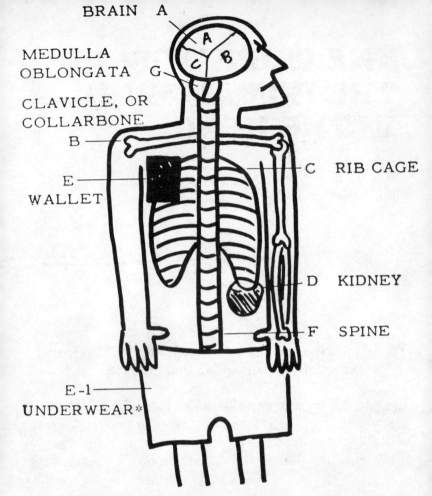

BRAIN A

MEDULLA OBLONGATA G

CLAVICLE, OR COLLARBONE B

E WALLET

C RIB CAGE

D KIDNEY

F SPINE

E-1 UNDERWEAR*

Because of its central location we shall consider first the spine (F). At the top the spine is connected to the base of the brain. At the bottom it disappears into the underwear. If it were not for the spine, when you sat down at dinner your head would fall forward into the soup.

* In anatomy class we had lady instructors.

The spine is connected to the most unlikely parts of the human body. It is connected by means of "nerves."

These nerves carry messages to the brain. This is vital, especially in times of an emergency. To illustrate, suppose a typical emergency occurs. Suppose you get your elbow stuck in a mustard jar (medium dark). Immediately the elbow sends a message up through the clavicle to the spine, which zips it on to the brain.

NORMAL ELBOW

ELBOW STUCK IN MUSTARD JAR
(Medium Dark)

The message says, "Help, I'm stuck in a mustard jar! Elbow. Over." But the brain, as we shall learn in a few pages, has more important things to worry about, so it sends a message back, saying, "Don't bother me; I'm busy thinking. Over and out."

This, naturally, induces a state of irritability in the elbow, which begins to fret and shift about inside the mustard jar. It sends another message to the brain, saying, "It's easy for you to say, 'Don't bother me,' but I'm the one that's stuck, and I think you should have a little consideration for others."

Then it sends another message, and another, and another.

These messages, unanswered, begin to pile up at the base of the brain around the *medulla oblongata* (G), and they form a block.

This block can cause a condition known as Water on the Brain. My cousin Bobble suffered very badly from this condition. See opposite page.

Bobble Before Surgery

I recognized Bobble's symptoms immediately (sloshing, gurgling) and tried everything to help him. I tried putting him under a sun lamp to bring him to a boil; I tried aspiring. Nothing worked so I took him to a surgeon who installed an overflow drain pipe in Bobble's head. (See page 44.)

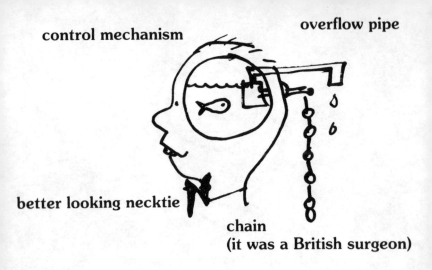

control mechanism

overflow pipe

better looking necktie

chain
(it was a British surgeon)

The operation worked fine (although afterwards Bobble wasn't invited to many parties), but eventually Bobble came to a bad end. One day when he was walking home from school he got his shoelace caught in the chain and flushed himself to death.

Now that we have that out of the way we can take up the Male Brain directly.

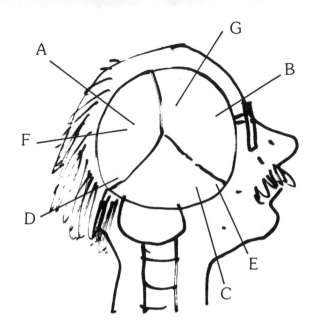

AVERAGE MALE BRAIN. With key (below) to the various areas and their function.

	AREA	**FUNCTION**
THALAMUS	A	Bad Temper
	B	Hollering
CEREBRUM	C	Sense of smell
	D	Vertical hold
	E	Contrast
CEREBELLUM	F	Angst
	G	Remembering gas tank cap after using Self-Service pump.

The functions above are properly known as the reflexive or autonomic functions. Actual thinking, contemplation and decision-making go on in the cortical "part" of the brain. Which is itself divided into three sub "parts." The uppermost "part," or libido (labeled U.P.) is devoted to thinking about:

Voyeurism	Groping
Pornography	Homosexuals
Bondage	Flashing
Orgies	Chickens
Rape	Self-Abuse
Masochism	Incest
Bestiality	Tap Dancing Naked
Whips and Chains	Wearing Women's Underwear
Leather Stuff	Prostitution
Rubber Stuff	Talking Dirty

The middle "part" of the brain, labeled M.P., is less complex. It is devoted to thinking about Doing "It."

There is always a conflict between the M.P. and the U.P. which leads to various male eccentricities such as yelling a lot and drunkenness.

The Bottom "part" of the brain, or B.P., is that highly popular area which concentrates exclusively on Money. Money is, to the male, second only in importance to "It." He reasons, correctly, that if he has a great deal of money he will be able to do "It" with a higher type of consenting adult.

THE FEMALE NERVOUS SYSTEM

I have spent an undue amount of time studying the female Nervous System, and continue to do so, and I have found that it is more capable of adjusting to stress than the male Nervous System. Because of this (probably), women can live longer than men, own more shares of AT&T and have fewer traffic accidents.

Actually, with the exception of throwing baseballs, lifting heavy weights and cooking, women can do most things better than men, including "It."

Women protect and preserve what we laughingly call civilization (ha ha ha). They create Order out of Chaos. Men, on the other hand, spend most of their time creating Chaos out of Order.

Neither of them ever quite make it, which is a Good Thing otherwise the world could become (1) a bloody mess or (2) absolutely perfect and either way it probably wouldn't be much fun.

Female Nervous System (Prone)

THE SCHWINE KITZENGER POLL AND TEST

All men's miseries come from their inability to sit quiet and alone.

—Blaise Pascal

If we are ever to have an Avoidist World Society we must do something about the problem of Thinking. Too much still goes on in spite of television, cocaine, alcohol, marijuana and amplified guitars.

Fortunately sociologists have provided us with an effective method which minimizes the need for Thought.

Throughout history the invention of a new weapon has always been followed by the discovery of a defense against the weapon. By the time they had the bugs out of the first bow and arrow, someone had thought up the Shield. The answer to gunpowder was armor plate. When the H-Bomb was perfected, Schizophrenia came along.

And when the Communists invented Brain Washing, the Democracies countered with the Public Opinion Poll.

The Poll protects us from the danger and effort of having to make up our own minds. If a citizen has to know his opinion about anything he can look it up quickly on a statistical chart. (See opposite page.)

And the best of all possible polls is the Schwine Kitzenger Poll. It is the only one that subscribes to all of the other polls and then swipes their stuff and reprints it.

Dr. Schwine and Dr. Kitzenger are specialists in public opinion and this is certainly an age of specialization. Would you try to generate your own electricity, smoke your own bacon, lay your own eggs? You wouldn't drill your own teeth or make your own phenobarbital, would you? Of course not!

So why should you try to make up your own mind when the Pollsters already know what you think? *Of course if you think you don't think what you are supposed to think you are an Eccentric Malcontent so who cares what you think?**

Here is the way the Polls work:

Suppose you want to know how you feel about Artichokes. In August, 1979, an unbiased survey was taken by NAG (the National Artichoke Grower's Gazette).

---

*When writing about polls, it is important to use undecipherable language to show you are an expert.

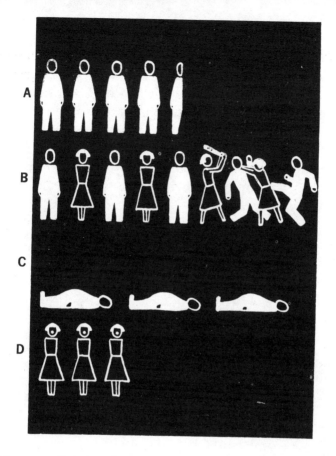

This excellently drawn chart shows (A) Percent of Males favoring Farm Price Support at 100% of Parity, (B) Adults with College Education in favor of aid to Peru, with Disagreement as to Method indicated at right, (C) Proportion of Males preferring three Martinis before lunch, (D) The Pointer Sisters.

First a sample group was selected, consisting of 100 NAG members who were carefully chosen to represent 200,000,000 Americans. (Sample Group selection is based on the scientific principal that "If one dog has spots, all dogs have spots," a premise originated simultaneously by Dr. Gallup and Idi Amin.)

The persons in the sample group were asked to answer the following question:

WHICH WOULD YOU RATHER DO? (a) EAT AN ARTICHOKE (b) HAVE POISON IVY ON THE BOTTOM OF YOUR FEET?

Of the 100 persons answering this question, 96 gave the (a) answer.

Trained statisticians then reduced this evaluation to a conclusion, namely:

"96% PREFER ARTICHOKES."
and a corollary:

"ARTICHOKES ARE 96% BETTER."

This information is then rushed to you so that you will know exactly how you feel about Artichokes.

NOTE: Occasionally, of course, a slip-up can occur. Last year Schwine and Kitzenger received a communication from An Average Male Eskimo who lived in Chakku, Alaska. This gentleman whose name was Johnny Sellrottenbeaverskintotradingpost, had a question:

"DID HE OR DID HE NOT LIKE WHALE BLUBBER?"

We surveyed this and found that persons in his ethnic group were crazy about whale blubber because:

1. IT IS NOURISHING.
2. IT CONTAINS VITAMIN B-12.
3. IT IS THE ONLY THING AVAILABLE FOR THEM TO EAT.

We wrote Mr. Sellrottenbeaverskintotradingpost to this effect but due to the infrequent mail service to Chakku, by the time he received our answer he had succumbed to malnutrition.

Now here are the results of the latest S-K survey. A team of interviewers consisting of Dr. Schwine, Dr. Kitzenger, Mrs. Schwine (who is in charge of interviewing people who don't want to be interviewed) and myself asked the following question on October 24, 1979:

"WHO DO YOU THINK SHOULD BE THE NEXT PRESIDENT OF THE UNITED STATES?"

Where Asked: In the hallways of the Eldridge Cleaver Junior High School in Northern California

SAMPLE USED: Scientifically selected loiterers

Candidate Preferred	Number Of Loiterers Preferring
Jimmy Carter	5
Billy Carter	11
Rosalynn Carter	38
Jerry Brown	23
Ted Kennedy	30
Valerie Perrine	45
Gilda Radner	101
Howard Cosell	1*
The Bee Gees	230
Myron McDoon	(none)

ANALYSIS: At first glance this poll might seem to indicate that Myron McDoon was running in last place. Not so. The trained pollster knows how to evaluate (i.e. outsmart) interviewees and knows that when stating a political preference people always name, not their real choice, but the opposition candidate whom they consider to be the weakest so as to give their own candidate a better chance on election day. When viewed from this professional standpoint the results obviously indicate a landslide for McDoon.

*This vote was obviously cast by a Carl Gassoway, Eccentric Malcontent, trying to be funny.

CONCLUSION: 96% prefer McDoon.

OVERALL TRENDS

Dr. Kitzenger is our specialist on Overall Trends and his latest report is that "More Overalls are worn by farmers than by City People."

By this time you should have a better appreciation of what Opinion Polls mean to you. Just remember, in all our national elections, the polls have been 100% infallibly correct (allowing a normal 50% margin for error, of course).

Early Avoidists

"THE BREAKTHROUGH"

"Nine times out of ten, in the arts as in life, there is no truth to discover, only error to be exposed."

—H.L. Mencken

Many people today keep busy pretending to be busy. They don't really want to finish a job or a project because then it could be judged. They would rather keep fooling around and talking a lot about the importance of what they are pretending to do. A corollary of this is the belief that it's more important to buy and own stuff than to use it, as witness all the expensive "food processors" that are like a family cat—pretty but useless.

The following brief fable (which came to me in a dream) is indicative of some future event that will undoubtedly happen someday.

Early Non-Avoidists

In the year 1985, a biochemist named Elvira Galk was employed in the research department of Universal Pharmaceuticals, Inc., known to the world as UNIPHAR. Elvira Galk's job was to develop new shades of fingernail polish. While so engaged she isolated the hormone which causes fingernails to regenerate themselves, to keep growing even after death.

She evolved an inexpensive method of synthesizing this hormone, and after a lengthy series of tests using laboratory mice, she concluded that if the Hormone were taken orally twice a day for six months, it would halt the aging process.

Elvira reported her discovery, through channels, to the UNIPHAR Planning Board and asked for permission to produce the Hormone in quantity. Members of the board were impressed and gave her an immediate answer:

"We will undertake a feasibility study."

Surveys were then made to determine the market potential for a product of this type.

The surveys showed a positive reaction on the part of the public. *Over 72% indicated they would like to live forever*.

Although UNIPHAR was a gigantic organization, in matters of this kind, it could move rapidly. It swung into action. Budgets were approved:

PRODUCTION BUDGET $65,850.25

ADVERTISING BUDGET $6,500,000.25

Creative people were called in to focus on the critical problem of a name.

Within a month, the Planning Board settled on the name "NO-GO." It was succinct. It described the product. It had a certain music. A package was designed.

And a nationwide campaign, utilizing all media, was laid out. Its purpose was to use psychology to create a desire for the new product.

Public response was immediate:

45,000,000 units were sold during the first eight days. The president of UNIPHAR sent a memo to the Planning Board: "I think we have something here. Full speed ahead."

There were, as could be expected, some adverse reactions.

"The idea of living forever is un-American. The Communist origins of such a plan should be exposed."

—Nat'l. Assoc. of Morticians

"This drug could cause widespread unemployment."
—Nat'l. Council of Churches

"Yew cain't make us take hit!"

— *Jehovah's Witness*

"I am categorically neither for nor against this marvelous product which then agin may help to stop inflation or sumpin'."

—*Jimmy Carter, ex-President*

"No-Go? I never trust none of them Chinamen."

—*Billy Carter*

"I vant some."

—*Z.Z. Gabor*

"It made my hair fall out."

— *lady in Davenport, Iowa*

"It cured my gallstones."

—*man in Vermont*

Several class action suits were started and the Federal Trade Commission issued a Cease and Desist order, claiming that the No-Go advertising campaign could not be substantiated.

"So far," the FTC's **Chief Counsel stated, " no one has lived forever."**

UNIPHAR produced four people who said they *had* lived forever, but the FTC countered by pointing out that two of these people had never taken No-Go.

The injunction was lifted, but legal wrangling continued; so did the Advertising and Promotion. Profits and gross sales rose higher and higher. And, of course, competitive products began to appear.

1. **ANTI-AGE, with improved fast-acting Bufferin**
2. **ETERNALEEN, improved low-calorie life capsule**
3. **EVER-HAPPY, in improved liquid form with 58% alcohol base.**
4. **SUPER-STUD, improved real he-man's life capsule.**
5. **TEEN-TERNA-LIFE, with improved Acne cure in six flavors.**

Each of these new products captured 17.5% of the market. No-Go itself soon became old-fashioned, outdated.

Then, a chiropractor in Teaneck, New Jersey, published a book called "Stuff Yourself Skinny" which stated that eating two pounds of stabilized fowl fat every day would cause loss of weight and eliminate unpleasant personal odors. The book, the theory and the diet were an instant success. 900,000 copies were sold the first week. The demand for stabilized fowl fat became enormous. It turned out that S.F.F. (as it came to be known) was chicken fat that had been treated personally by the chiropractor in Teaneck, N.J.

When 4,000,000 copies of the book were sold the second week, UNIPHAR bought the secret stabilizing process from the chiropractor in Teaneck and began marketing Stabilized Fowl Fat pills.

77,000,000 pills were sold the first four days.

The sales of No-Go dropped to .04% of the market. And then to .004%. The UNIPHAR Planning Board voted to concentrate their considerable energies on the S.F.F. Pills and they remaindered their No-Go inventory to the J.C. Penney Stores which sold a one-week supply for 19 cents.

The No-Go formula was then sold to a UNIPHAR subsidiary in Detroit (providing a profitable tax loss) and the subsidiary, which manufactured dog food, added the formula to a new line called "PERMA-PET."

CONCLUSION: One of these days some of the junk they sell us may really work, but no one will ever know. And if you are an Avoidist, you won't care.

Rare view (unretouched) of Miss Patricia Del Ray ("MISS AVOIDISM" for 1978, 1979, 1980)

MENTAL TREATMENTS NOW IN USE

My method is to take the utmost trouble to find the right thing to say, and then to say it with the utmost levity.

—G. Bernard Shaw

TREATING a person for mental aberration in this day and age is like giving a drowning man artificial respiration without taking him out of the lake. Things have become too confused. Treatment is not my answer. (Several letters have been received by the publishers from a Dr. Carl Gassoway demanding that I state that treatment is *his* answer. I have no intention of complying with this imbecilic request.)

In recent years, actually since the stock market retreat in 1974, a great many curious Programs and Systems devoted to helping the Copeless have achieved publicity and popularity. They include Reichianism, Esalen, est, Rev. Moon, Holistic Diets, Christianity (formerly a religion, now reclassified), Rolfing, Primal Therapy, Hare Krishna, Yoga, etc.

The more popular of these feature such fun programs as the Loving Love Center, Nude Body Reading, Sexual Psychodrama, Group Fondling, Co-ed Massage Classes and Self-Abuse as an Art Form. All have one thing in common: They cost money and have become big business!

But then so have politics, jogging, astrology, hamburger making and picture framing.

Everything that exists today is Big Business.

And the biggest and oldest business in the Self-Help Game is ANALYSIS.

There are several kinds of analysis including Transactional, Hypno- and Urin-. But the most orthodox, the oldest and the most popular is still Psycho-.

> *Psychoanalysis is a method of treating Copelessness and what used-to-be-called Neurosis (now known as "Bad Vibes") by forcing the patients to talk about themselves until they forget what was originally wrong with them.*

The American Medical Association has come out strongly in favor of Psychoanalysis. They give two principal reasons for their stand:
1. *It costs a lot.*
2. *It goes on and on and on and on and on.*

THE SCHWINE METHOD: HOW IT WORKS

There are several approaches to psychotherapy, but for the Avoidist, there is really only one: The "Schwine" method devised by the eminent scientist, Albert Schwine. About this method the eminent authority, J. Taylor Dorsey, M.D., has said:

> "... Sure-fire! A crackerjack system. Results gotten first time. A guaranteed money-maker."

The Schwine Method has one tremendous advantage for the would-be therapist. It requires no diploma.

At the present time the Schwine Method is being used by only one practitioner, my maternal uncle, J. Taylor Dorsey.

The Schwine Method requires little equipment: a couch, a desk, a chair, a pad of notepaper and a good lawyer.

When a new patient consults Dr. Dorsey, the procedure is as follows. After a preliminary examination of the patient's Heredity, Social Attitudes and Marital Status, Dr. Dorsey tells him, her, or it to go home and write a complete history of his, her or its life, putting in every detail, no matter how embarrassing or libelous. Dr. Dorsey then reads the patient's history, corrects the grammar as best he can, changes a few names, and submits it to *The National Enquirer*.

You will notice that the chair in Dr. Dorsey's office is placed behind the couch (Fig. below) so that the patient cannot see the therapist. This is so that once the patient begins talking, Dr. Dorsey can sneak out the door,[†] telephone friends, and take care of customers in his haberdashery downstairs.

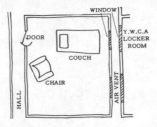

OTHER METHODS/ SHOCK TREATMENT

Recommended for advanced cases. This method requires a great deal of complicated equipment, which passes 10,000 volts of electricity (higher west of the Rockies) through the patient's body. The equipment may either be purchased or constructed at home with an A.C. Gilbert Number 3 Mister Science Kit.

†See Sigmund Freud, *The Use of the Tennis Shoe in Psychoanalysis* (1930).

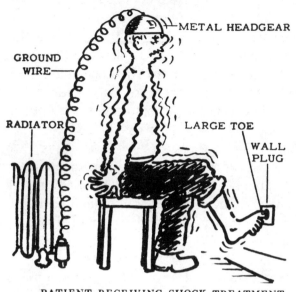

GROUND WIRE

METAL HEADGEAR

RADIATOR

LARGE TOE

WALL PLUG

PATIENT RECEIVING SHOCK TREATMENT

WATER TREATMENT

This treatment consists of plunging the patient rapidly into alternate tubs of hot and cold water. It is recommended for dirty patients.

THEMATIC APPERCEPTION

These T.A.T. tests have been widely used by many so-called psychologists to determine the "Type" of personality breakdown a patient may be undergoing. The most efficient, in my opinion, is the Schwine Kitzenger Test. The Schwine Kitzenger Test was designed by Dr. Albert Schwine and Dr. Otto Kitzenger, who came from opposite schools of psychological thought. Actually Schwine and Kitzenger had only one thing in common— Mrs. Schwine.

The Schwine Kitzenger Test was an imaginative extension of the Rorschach Test. But instead of analyzing ink blots, S. and K. would have the subject come into the office and sit down on a fried egg. Then, they would analyze the seat of his trousers.

This was messy but profitable, particularly since Kitzenger ran a cleaning and pressing establishment in the building.

In the light of present-day knowledge, the results seem crude, but then, we must remember, so do Schwine and Kitzenger.

Of minimal interest are the following samples of Schwine Kitzenger Test analyses reprinted by permission of The American Poultryman's Journal, April 13, 1970. Fried eggs.

Fried egg
before test

Subject untrust-
worthy: sits
down sideways

Subject cautious:
very careful
sitter

Subject is fat

(Scale 1/10th actual size)

One other test was quite ingenious, although it only worked in analyzing male patients. Schwine and Kitzenger would take the subject and lock him in a room with a Ms. Patricia Del Ray. In one wall of the room was a two-way mirror and, once the subject was locked in, Schwine and Kitzenger would peep through the mirror and study what went on. Occasionally they would invite scientifically minded friends to peep through the mirror with them. The tests attracted so much interest that they were able to raise the prices three times in one six-month-period.

They finally gave up this test, however, because of an accident. One evening the bleachers Kitzenger had put up collapsed and 14 members of the Elks Club were almost killed.

OCCUPATIONAL THERAPY
CASE OF THOMAS ALVA EDISON*

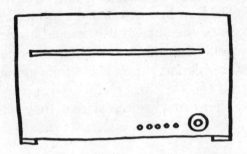

When Thomas Alva Edison was born he was a normal healthy child but his mother always thought he was sickly. She kept taking his temperature. Whenever she thought of it she would shove a thermometer into his little mouth. Then she would forget about it. Thomas Alva would chew the ends off the thermometers and swallow the mercury. By the time he was 7 he had swallowed the mercury out of 231 thermometers. That year they had a very hot summer. By June 20th, Thomas Alva was 9 feet tall.

His tendency toward vertical vacillation made him nervous and when he was 21 he came to me for help. I told him to take up a hobby such as electronics. He did and almost immediately he invented a remarkable television set. It had a screen one inch high and 63 inches long. It was for people who squint.

*Fictitious name used to protect identity of patient.

CONCLUSION

These are merely a few of the current techniques being used, unsuccessfully, to treat Copelessness.

There are other treatments, of course, and in 1978 my Grandfather Tooten began work on a comprehensive 12-volume anthology that would include all of the known facts about all of the known techniques.

Unfortunately, he couldn't get a new ribbon for his typewriter so he quit and started raising rabbits instead.

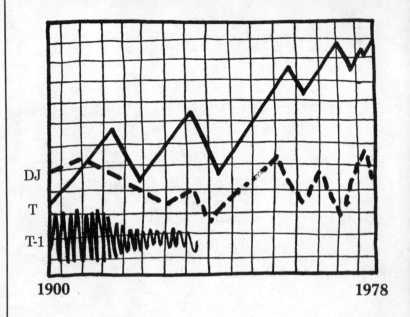

In the above graph, the line "T" shows the increase in talk per capita from 1900 to 1978. It is increasing 44% more rapidly than the Dow Jones Industrial Average (line "DJ").

The second line, "T-1" is where I was getting a sharp point on my pencil. (It's murder trying to draw a good graph with a dull pencil, and it's hard to keep a pencil sharpened around here as Sloan has childishly hidden all the sharpeners. Well, he hasn't really *hidden* them but he has taken them with him and locked himself in his office.)

CONVERSATIONAL AVOIDING

*Ask not what your country can do for you,
but what more your country can do for you.*

—J. Taylor Dorsey

No subject affords greater opportunities for study, or promises richer rewards, than Conversational Avoiding. Because conversation (i.e. the listening part) is directly related to one of society's greatest problems: *Understanding!*

Listening to other people leads to Understanding Them. And this leads to more emotional problems than you could shake a snake at.

Think about it. Who do you really dislike? Some stranger in Wichita Falls, Montana? No. The people we really dislike are those we understand. Our families, parents, sisters, brothers, uncles, aunts . . . our bosses, the people we see every day at work. There must be an end to these constant and successful attempts to "understand each other."

One of the ways to overcome this *Understanding Explosion* is to stop listening. This isn't easy. According to H.H. van Dester of Yale University, "People talk too much."

Because of this volume of talk (see page 76) that floods western civilization, the Beginning Avoidist will sometimes be trapped into Paying Attention. There is a danger here of becoming involved in something—probably more listening—and the following rule should be obeyed when possible: THE GOOD AVOIDIST NEVER PAYS ATTENTION.

Whenever this sort of danger threatens (or any other time you feel like it), you may Avoid by employing five Tested Remarks of such extreme dullness that the Avoidee will experience a partial paralysis lasting approximately four minutes. These remarks are:

1. A girl I used to go with when I was in high school just got a job with the Telephone Company.
2. I got this suit three years ago in Pittsburgh for 50 dollars.
3. I went to bed real early last night, but I didn't go to sleep until after midnight.
4. I sure wish I'd kept up with my piano lessons when I was a kid.
5. I can take better pictures with a little Instamatic than I can with those real expensive cameras.

(Note: When traveling, the following may be substituted for No. 5: "I used to live down that street.")

THE AVOIDIST PET

Despite a multimillion dollar promotional effort the three networks were unable to persuade Americans to watch the November elections. In New York, for example, nearly 70% of the audience tuned to the "Pink Panther" movie.

— *from ESQUIRE MAGAZINE, Jan. '79*

One of the problems that the beginning Avoidist often has is loneliness. We are all conditioned to think that having people around is the same as "having fun" and, like most Americans, we believe that *not* having *fun* is somehow immoral and un-American.

So in the withdrawal period between your Activist, busy life and your future, happy, catatonic, Avoidistic life, we suggest that you acquire a little pet.

Pets today are BIG BUSINESS. (The very fact that these two words can describe so many things referred to in this book is a great argument in favor of Avoidism.)

But you must exercise great caution in choosing a pet. Believe me, when they saturate prime time with commercials for seven-flavored cat food and gourmet goodies for doggies, you can bet there are a lot of people out there trying to get you *involved*. More money is spent on pet food in America than is spent on the education of children through the age of 12. *Billions* of dollars are spent on Booties for Beagles, Deodorants for Doxies, Combs for Kinkajous and Bikinis for Guppies.

Avoid any pet that is the center of an Industry.
The only proper pet for the true Avoidist is the Clam.

PET CLAMS

I became interested in clams as pets after I conducted the series of tests on my cousin Clarence, noted in Chapter 1. This clam, although beaten decisively in the tests, remained affectionate and friendly. These qualities, you will find, are typical of the entire phylum Mollusca.

Owning a pet Clam can open up a new way of life—a healthier, more fulfilling way of life.

You can lavish affection and love on a Clam. You can also hate the clam, call it names, argue politics with it, get rid of all your miserable hostilities.

But no matter what—the Clam will always respect and admire you. It will never criticize, turn sulky or try to borrow money.

CHOOSING A CLAM

Following are four of the breeds most popular with American Clam Lovers. In choosing your pet, pick one that suits your particular needs.

—QUAHOG STEAMER *(lamellibranchia arenaria)* Ch. Prince Henry of Odin

This is Buck, my first show Clam, photographed while being judged in a 1965 Bivalve Competition. Although they have a tendency to chase cars, the Quahogs have a reputation for being excellent Watch Clams.

—CHERRYSTONE *(Venus mercenaria)*

My Own Brucie VI Call name: "Brucie."

Particularly important in judging a Show Cherrystone is good posture. Notice Brucie's excellent stance, the rounded muzzle and delicate cryptodon.

81

—TOY LITTLE NECK *(Mya truncata)*
Ch. Royal Gloamshire Lady, my own
Shirley of Streatham. Call name: "Royal
Gloamshire Lady, my own Shirley of
Streatham."

The Toy Little Neck, very popular with apartment dwellers, makes an excellent companion for children. It enjoys nothing better than a good romp and will never, even in fun, clack at a Little One.

Ch. Roger's Ventilator Shaft of 88th Street
West Near Walden School. Call name:
"Spike."

Spike, though only a whelp, already exhibits the tenacity, courage and affinity for nicotine common to his breed. In field trials for Working Clams held last summer at Coney Island he placed second in plankton tracking and retrieving.

THE CARE AND FEEDING OF PET CLAMS

Diet: You should feed your Clam once a day. It will thrive on almost any kind of goop you have around the house (corn flakes, coffee grounds, newspaper) although most *prefer* Breast of Capon Stroganoff with a tossed green salad served with a light moselle wine.

Grooming: The Clam, with its clean habits, requires little grooming. Give it a daily polish with a piece of sandpaper. Swab its siphon out once a week with a piece of cotton dipped in horseradish. You will not need to bathe your Clam.

Clam diseases: If your Clam turns black, becomes soft and starts to stink up the house, it is merely trying to tell you it is not feeling well. In fact, it probably has vascular Filibranchia, more commonly known as "the Poop." Pry its shell open with a hammer and chisel and squeeze half a lemon on its stomach. If this doesn't help, soak it in lye and use it for a Monopoly Counter.

Buck responding to back scratching.

Brucie and Friend Playing in kennel.

The Clam loves to show off and with patience can be taught many tricks, the best of which are Guarding and Playing Dead. However, training requires firmness. You must remember always to reward your Clam when he succeeds by saying, "Good Mollusk. Good Boy," and if he fails you must hit him with a mallet.

AVOIDIST SCIENCE

The federal government spends Eight Billion Dollars a year on paper alone.

— From Jan. 14, 1979 "60 Minutes"

A Provocateur in the pay of the large corporations named Dr. Carl Gassoway has sent me six Mailgrams stating that there can be no Avoidist Science because Science is based upon activity. The Mailgrams also contained other statements, equally absurd, which related to my personal life. I am ignoring them and him. Because there certainly is an Avoidist science. Avoidism and Science can at times produce a synergism such as the *new* and *improved* atomic bomb which I personally invented.

I hit upon the principle for this bomb a few years ago when I read an article about energy in the National Enquirer which was illustrated with photos of Lee Marvin's feet. I am now prepared to release the details of this bomb. I trust you will not mail them (the details) to anyone behind the "Iron Curtain."*

*Russia

But first a little background on atomic and subatomic structure.

Everything is made of atoms: air, wood, buildings, water, Cheryl Ladd, veal scallopini and Toledo, Ohio, are all just piles of atoms. Here we have a diagram of the atom used in the first successful demonstration of fission in 1940.

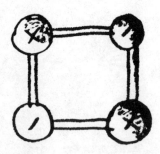

URANIUM 140. Composed of two linked positive electrical charges and four negative charges.

This atom was subjected to tremendous pressure and to a temperature of 4000 degrees Centigrade (note charred edges at right). This caused two of the negative charges to disappear, which altered the structure of the Uranium and turned it into something entirely different: Liverwurst. When this experiment was first performed at the University of California, it started a chain reaction. All over the State, scientists started opening up delicatessen stores.

Here we have diagrams of other atoms. Study them carefully so you will recognize them in everyday life.

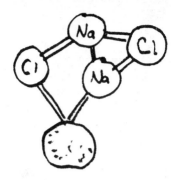

SALT: (NaCl) A molecule of sodium surrounded by two molecules of chlorine and a lump caused by dampness.

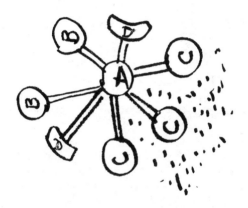

MINESTRONE SOUP: A positive nucleus surrounded by electrons and protons, carrot slices and parmesan cheese.

Now that you have some background, I will explain my new superior fission bomb. I say it is superior because it has one great advantage over any other type of atomic bomb so far developed. It is harmless.

It is amazing that no one has ever thought of this before, but that's the way it is with great discoveries. The idea is right there under everyone's nose until some unusually smart person just happens to stumble on it.

The Avoidist Bomb is also silent which can save us a lot of money as Public Libraries can be used for testing.

The fissionable material in the bomb is Lint 235. It works like this.(I would appreciate it if, after reading the following, you would rip out this page and eat it.) Two hemispheres of Lint 235 are snapped smartly together with a giant rubber band causing the Lint 235 to break down into Lint 233 and Fuzz 230. Although harmless in the accepted sense, the Lint bomb can cause trouble if you are wearing a blue serge suit. (If the page has a pulpy taste, try wrapping it around a hot dog coating it with mustard.)

AVOIDIST SEX

"After the age of 35 men should sleep with women in order to keep them around; they should not think that they are keeping them around to sleep with them."

—*Old folk saying*

The very idea of sex is, of course, distasteful to the Avoidist. It represents so much that we have fought against, but it is difficult nowadays to avoid this troublesome area of pseudo-athletic activity which has become one of America's largest cottage industries. And under its commercial name, Pornography, it is one of the country's biggest businesses.

Pornography, proliferates like sunflowers over a leaky cesspool. Pornographic movies and magazines have given new meaning to the pejorative term "Jerk." There are Porn T-Shirts, Porn Motels, Porn People, Porn Mickey Mouse Dolls and probably Porn Mah Jong Tiles.

We cannot honestly expect you to avoid sex, but you can minimize your participation and take steps to guarantee that in any sexual relationship you will end up as the Avoidist not the Avoidee.

I have spent a good part of my life studying sex with the help of four wives and others. And I am not loath to passing along knowledge I have gained from experience. It is, of course, experience from the male viewpoint, but this will be doubly interesting to females as it will give them a hitherto unsuspected perspective on themselves and their actions.*

In this area today Male Avoidists are faced with a greater problem than ever before. Many contemporary females feel themselves to be so Sexually Liberated that they have taken the initiative and view men the way 6th Century Romans viewed Sabine Women. They have realized that the Hounds have more fun than the Fox and have become . . . *aggressive*.

While this may seem titillating at first, the long-term implications could be disastrous to (a) the Male Ego, (b) the Male health, and (c) the Avoidist Movement. Steps must be taken.

Some Tips for the Male, Designed to Discourage the Sexually Liberated Female Without Insulting or Alienating Her.

Since advice of this kind has not been previously available it is important to proceed cautiously.

---

*(EDITORIAL NOTE: This is in no way true. Mr. Price insists on putting in this kind of dumb statement in order to "please my many, many female fans" . . . as he puts it. L. Sloan.)

So let us begin with a few DON'TS. Do not, repeat *not*, say:
—"I just had my hair done."
—"I don't want to ruin a perfect evening."
—"I can't. I'm having my period."
These excuses will not work.

Following are some positive approaches for avoiding an eager partner. Study them carefully.

1. NO ROOM AT THE INN. If the sexually liberated female, or SLF, has no place of her own, your problem is simplified. Tell her that you would like to invite her to your place, but you share it with four airline pilots. Because of their odd schedules one of them is always up and around.

2. USE OF DRUGS. Assuming (1) doesn't work and it probably won't, you will find yourself and the Liberated Lady alone at your place. Try to slip a little something in her drink. Preferably a crushed Valium or a Seconal tablet. If, with the help of soft music, you can lull her to sleep even for a few minutes, you have it made.

When she wakes up you can easily imply that something went on.

SELF: "Boy, Estelle, you really are a Tiger. Where did you learn those positions?"

HER: "Huh?"

SELF: "You sure know how to please a man . . . er . . . person, that is."

HER: "Yeah??"

SELF: "Took a lot out of me. Four times is usually my limit. Wow!"

HER: ". . . Wow?????"

3. DISABILITY (Minor). Whereas a "headache" has long been a feminine diversionary device, it isn't suitable for men. However, a backache is. At dinner move with great caution. With practice you can take as long as seven minutes just to slide into a booth in a restaurant.

HER: "What in the world is wrong with you?"

SELF: "Played eight games of Racquet Ball after work. I think I sprung my back again. It'll be okay tomorrow as long as I don't move around too much."

4. DISABILITY (Major). If the situation is beginning to get hairy, come right out and tell the Female that you cannot function because (a) you just had a vasectomy and it hasn't healed yet, or (b) you converted to Judaism and recently had a circumcision. Many SLFs will be suspicious and/or intrigued by this and may want to

check out your disability. It is advisable to give verisimilitude to the ploy by the use of a well-placed Band-Aide.

SELF: "See, Sweetheart, I wasn't kidding."
HER: "Hey, that is interesting."
SELF: "Owwwwwww. Estelle, don't *do* that."

5. THE BRUCE BIT. Pretend to go along with the SLF's plans. Embrace her passionately. Kiss her and hum tenor. Breathe audibly through the nose (a deviated septum is a big help here). Then when you presumably have reached the limit of your control, bury your face in her hair and murmur hoarsely, "Bruce, Bruce." This should get you off the hook and the Lady can't get peeved at you without appearing to be a chauvinist.

6. ANTI-APHRODISIACS. Some girls are Turned Off by specifics such as clothing, scents and expressions. For instance, wearing white lisle socks with black shoes will work as often as not. Few women are so depraved that will attempt to seduce a man wearing white lisle socks and black shoes.

Eating raw garlic is okay unless the SLF is Italian or a Food Faddist.

Say "Okey-dokey" a lot.

7. GOD IS WATCHING. Decorate your home with religious objects: crucifixes, pictures of Jesus with moving eyes, Madonnas, Mezuzahs, Buddahs, fonts of Holy Water. An autographed picture of one or more Popes will help. In such an atmosphere of sanctity it

should not be hard to convince the SLF that although you have great desire for her, you are dedicated to a higher cause.

8. INSTANT ALLERGY. Up until the actual moment of contact you can safely go along with the SLF's game plan. Then when she throws herself on, across, under and/or over you, flinch and begin scratching all over with both hands.

SELF: "My God, Estelle, it's my allergy. What kind of toothpaste do you use?"

9. BEDROOM SNEAK. Plead a deadline and pressures of work that must be gotten into the office by tomorrow morning and tell the SLF to go to bed. "I'll be right there just as soon as I knock out this little ol' report."

Then turn out the light and go into the front room (or the john) and read a Ross MacDonald book until her regular breathing tells you she is asleep. Read another half hour to be sure. Then take off your clothes and tip-tip-tippy-toe to the bed as quiet as a mouse. Pull back the sheet and slide ever so gently under it all at once, so as not to jiggle the mattress.

Unfortunately, at this writing no human male has ever been able to move softly enough to get into bed without waking up a horny female. Within a matter of seconds, you will find that a soft, pink, warm little arm has flopped over and given you a grab. At this point begin snoring loudly.

10. THE FULL FREAKOUT. The moment you are inside your apartment push the SLF onto the sofa and rush into the bedroom. Take off your shoes and socks and emerge wearing a long leather coat and carrying a giant bull-whip in one hand and a length of chain in the other. Assume a lecherous crouch (study Groucho in old Marx Brothers films) and stalk around the sofa humming basso profundo. At this point the SLF should remember an early morning appointment.

But be wary. This technique can be dangerously counter-productive in that it may (a) frighten the SLF away forever or (b) intrigue her. If the latter is the case, *do not, under any circumstances, let her get her hands on the bull-whip.*

When appropriately applied, these techniques should be of assistance in Avoiding Libidinal Involvement. If they don't—well, you can put the failure down to your innate irresistible charm. Why not?

Tips for the Female
I'm sorry to say that I have no Tips for Females. All of them that I have ever known have been natural Avoidists in the sexual field. They have evasive maneuvers developed in ancient times (before 1960) such as the Headache, the Period and the Hairdo (see above). If by chance any of these do not work you might try asking the Inflamed Male to lend you money. Or wear white lisle socks with black shoes.

SEXUAL AVOIDING (WRONG)

SOME GENERAL
LOOSE ENDS
As of 1979

Looking back I find that I have overlooked several subjects and a number of items that I planned to say something instructive about. For instance:

INFLATION
An interesting subject. In an effort to learn more about it I recently traveled over a thousand miles to see Dr. Milton Friedman, the economist in Chicago. But he was out to lunch.

GOATS
Goats are gentle and affectionate creatures. They should not be confused with Groats which are whole grain buckwheat.

WHITE SHIRTS
There are not enough of these around.

CARTERS
There are too many of these around.

LITERARY STYLE
While editing this manuscript, the publishers insisted violently that I cut out a number of words. There is nothing wrong with any of these words, so far as I can see, and I shall include them here in case you have any use for them. They are no good to me now.

These are the words:

Very, very, very, very, very, very, very, very, Very, Very, VERY, very, very, very, Very, VERY, very, very, Very, Very, very, very, very, very, very, very, very, very, Very, VERY, very, very, very, very, very.

But now, but now, but now, but now, but now, but now, But now, But Now, but now, but now, But now, BUT NOW, but now, but now, BUT now, but now, But now, now but, Now but, now but, now but, now, now, now, now, now, But, but, but, but, but, but now, but, now, now, now, Now but.

As a matter of fact, as a matter of fact, as a matter of fact, As a Matter of Fact, as a matter of fact, as a matter of *fact*, as a matter of fact.

I, I, I, I, I, I, I, I, I, I, I, I, I, I, I, I, I, I, I, I, I, I, I, I, I, I, I, I, I, I, I, I, I, I, I, I, I, I, I, I, I, I, I, I, I, I, I, me, me, me, me, Roger Price, me, myself, myself, myself, myself, Myself, Me, me, ME, ME, ME, me, myself, Roger Price, R. Price, Roger Price, ROGER PRICE, R. Price, me, I, I, I, I, me, Roger Price.

However, However, However, However, however, however, however, however, however, however.

Miss Patricia Del Ray, Miss Patricia Del Ray, Miss Patricia Del Ray.

Royalties.

ENEMIES OF THE MOVEMENT

Last month a certain Dr. Carl Gassoway slipped into the P/S/S offices during lunch hour and dropped marbles down the washbasin drain and bent the blades on the electric fan. We have reason to believe that this is the same Dr. Carl Gassoway who, in 1978, poured emery dust into the hinges of the incinerator door in the Research Lab. This man has done everything possible to destroy the movement. Unfortunately, we have not been able to prove anything against him in court, but our investigators have disclosed an unusual fact. It seems that this Dr. Gassoway has been married for a number of years to Miss Patricia Del Ray (her business name). For some reason, this Dr. Gassoway has developed an unreasoning hostility toward myself, J. Taylor Dorsey, Schwine and Kitzenger, my grandfather Tooten, and, most recently, the Editor.

We are making plans to take care of this "crackpot."

He and his followers—Gassowayites—had better watch out.

FINAL LOOSE END (CONCLUSION)

By now you know almost everything that I know about everything. (If you don't, take a cold shower and read the book over again.) Knowing what you do, you have no excuse for not becoming an Avoidist. Right away. Some people may tell you that you should avoid Avoidism and should never have read this book. These people don't understand the philosophy and are just trying to be funny.

Take advantage of everything you've learned here. You are part of a bold experiment. You now have the "don't-know-how." It's up to you to use it. Do not put off putting off things until tomorrow. *Put them off today.* If you are tempted to lose faith, always remember that we here at GAD headquarters are behind you. Keep your chin down and a loose upper lip.

pss!®